Why Precious the Cat "Owns" a Retirement Home

PAGE PUBLISHING
Conneaut Lake, PA

First originally published by Page Publishing 2024

ISBN 979-8-89315-849-6 (pbk)
ISBN 979-8-89315-862-5 (digital)

Why Precious the Cat "Owns" a Retirement Home

Bette Stead

Well, come on in, and I'll tell you *why*. But first, I want to tell you more about my life and what led me to own a retirement home.

I was born in a medium-sized town in southeast Texas. My mother decided to have me and my four brothers and sisters in an old garage that wasn't used anymore. Some old boards were standing against the walls. She found a place behind a couple of old boards, which was big enough to make a nest.

There was a nice grassy yard nearby. So when we opened our eyes and could walk better, we went out there to exercise. I had blue eyes, long hair, and was fluffy. A human neighbor saw me one day and decided to adopt me. She was my Aunt Lucy, and her niece was Bette.

When Aunt Lucy first brought me into her house, I was dirty and had lots of fleas. She decided to give me a bath in shallow water in the bathtub. I hated it and yelled my head off. But Aunt Lucy had to do it and got me nice and clean. She dried me off with a bath towel and laid me on a dry bath towel on the bed. I was so exhausted, I immediately went to sleep and slept for over an hour.

She was trying to decide on a name for me. When friends came to visit, they would all look at me and say, "Aw, isn't that precious." That happened time after time. So Aunt Lucy finally said, "OK, that's *Precious.*" So that's how I got my name.

One day my human family decided it was time to move to another apartment about six blocks away. A mover came and took everything to our new home. I stayed on a neighbor's back porch. When it was time for me to move, I was put in a box with some air holes on the sides. The family didn't own a car, so Bette had to carry me in the box. Well, I didn't like that either, so I yelled a lot. Bette kept telling me that a sign of intelligence is the ability to adjust. I'd had enough of that box, so adjusting to it was out of the question.

I really liked the new apartment, as it was upstairs. I could lie in the window with just the screen behind me and have a good view. One day it snowed, which was the first time in ten years. Bette decided to take me outside to see the snow. She put me down on the ground. The snow was cold and wet, so I ran under the house to get away from it. Bette was horrified and begged me to come out. Finally, she went upstairs and got a piece of hamburger meat and coaxed me out. Luckily, she never showed me snow again!

Being brought up by Aunt Lucy and Bette, I was a cat of faith. I saw how they went to church, always said prayers, and helped other people. So I knew it was time for me to find a way to show my faith. We moved to a bigger city, and I was able to get out and explore. They put a collar on me with my name on it so all our new friends would know my name was Precious.

I came to a large building that looked like a hotel. The valets at the front door were very nice and let me in. It turned out to be a retirement home. As I walked around, people spoke to me and said, "Aw, isn't that cute." So I guess my long fur and pretty tail attracted them. I wanted to visit, so I scratched on a door. The residents opened the door and let me in. They seemed glad to see me and talked with me a while. Then they opened the door and said, "Good night," so I left. There were many comfortable places for me to sleep, and there were sofas in the living room areas of the building. I even sniffed out the kitchen and was given food and some milk.

Everyone was so nice to me that I decided to stay a while. I found out the residents could live in independent living, assisted living, mental health care, or health care. So I visited all these areas, and people seemed glad to see me. I was finally feeling like I was being a cat of faith. I now wanted to meet everyone there, but it was a ten-story building, and I knew that would take a while.

I went home to Aunt Lucy and Bette and told them what I had been doing and how happy the people at the retirement home seemed to see me. They could see how happy I was and that I was trying to spread happiness, so they said I could stay as long as I wanted. They hoped I would visit them once in a while. I guaranteed them that I would visit, as I had always loved them.

So I returned to the retirement home, and the residents and staff were obviously glad I was back. I began my plan of meeting everyone there. So I scratched on several doors a day.

One day a couple came to the door. They were *so happy* to see me and invited me right away. They told me their story. They had a cat that they loved and adored for twenty years, and he had passed away about a year ago. They both loved to pet him and missed him so much. So they petted me for a while, and I promised I would certainly remember them and visit them again as often as possible.

A few people there had cats and dogs. They were always polite to me too. One day I scratched at a door, and I couldn't believe my eyes. A big cat came to the door. He introduced himself and invited me in. He told me he had grown up in a fraternity house! I guess it was a good thing that he became a big cat. I guess I was rude, but I just had to ask him how much he weighed. He didn't seem to mind and told me seventeen pounds. He said he enjoyed being held, but his owner couldn't lift him. He had to jump up on the sofa beside her and climb into her lap to be held like a baby.

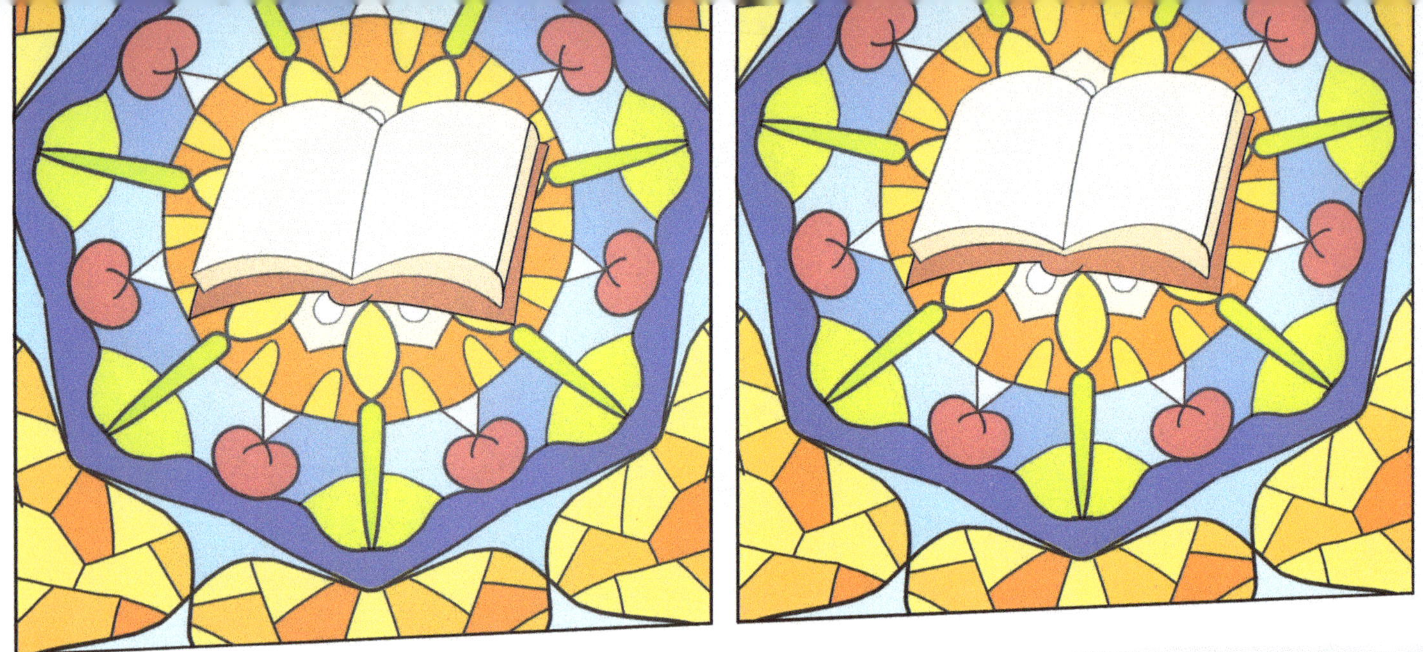

We have other great facilities here. As a cat of faith, I really love the chapel. It has stained-glass windows and is always open. On Sundays, they show a church service on the big screen. The service is from a nearby church, where a number of our residents are members. During the week, clergy will come and say prayers in our assisted living, mental health care, and health care areas. I am allowed to go to the chapel any time to attend services or just to pray. I also attend the prayers in the assisted living, mental health care, and health care areas. There is a church directly across the street from us where a lot of our residents are members. Some just walk across the street. It is a very busy street, so I worry about them. There is a stoplight, which helps a lot. I have never been there, as I can't seem to get up my courage to cross a busy street.

We have a very nice dining room where we can have meals and visit with different residents who become our friends. The service staff works very hard to meet our needs. Our swimming pool is used for exercise led by our excellent exercise director. One day a yellow-crowned night heron landed there. He was so beautiful, and we all told him we loved him and would feed him if he stayed. But unfortunately, he didn't stay very long. We also have places where residents can get pedicures, manicures, haircuts and blow-dries with curls, and physical therapy. The physical therapy staff is excellent. They are well-educated in their profession. There is a business office with a very smart lady who can help you with finances. She can also weigh a big envelope of papers and sell you the postage, so all you have to do is stick the postage on the envelope and drop it in the mailroom. We're so glad we have a good office for our executive director. He takes such good care of us and our needs. He also keeps up with building maintenance, which is always so important.

Our community center looks out to our great yard. There is a putting green and a fenced-off area for a dog run. There is also a beautiful huge tree, which is named Big Teddy.

Our Residents' Association meets monthly in the community center. Many residents attend to get news about our retirement home and to ask questions. I always attend and sit on the floor next to the stage.

One day, the president of the Residents' Association motioned to me at the beginning of the meeting to come over to the speaker's lectern, so I did. The president picked me up and put me on top where the microphone and gavel are. I took my paw and tapped on the gavel. Then I put my nose to the microphone and told the residents and staff who were present how grateful I was for all of their kindness to me. Of course, I had to use cat language, and I so hoped they would understand. I guess they did understand.

First, a resident shouted, "*Precious owns us!*" Then "*Precious owns us!*" was shouted all over the room! I was astonished. Everyone wanted to come up and pet me. I recognized that being a cat of faith had made all this happen.

Later that day, I went to tell Aunt Lucy and Bette what had happened. They were so very proud of me. They told me how much they love me and said to keep up the good work. I also told them that I loved them very much and would come back to visit often. As a cat of faith, I now have found my way.

About the Author

Bette Ann Stead is professor emerita at the C. T. Bauer College of Business, University of Houston (UH), where she taught for thirty-four years. She has published in the *Academy of Management Journal*, *IEEE Transactions on Engineering Management*, *Journal of Business Ethics*, *Information and Optimization Sciences*, *Journal of Library Administration*, *Vital Speeches of the Day*, and others. In 2004, she was named a Distinguished Alumna by Lamar University, and in 2011 she was the first woman named to the Lamar University College of Business Hall of Fame.

She established the Greater Houston Business Ethics Roundtable (GHBER) to highlight the pivotal role of ethics in the workplace and to share best practices. In 2006, on GHBER's tenth anniversary, five $1,000 scholarships were named in her honor. She wrote a proposal for a capital campaign and is now recognized as the architect of the capital campaign proposal that culminated in C. T. Bauer's $40 million endowment of the University of Houston's College of Business Administration.

Her awards include the Distinguished Faculty Member Award from the C. T. Bauer College of Business Alumni Association and the Mayor's Volunteer Houston Award for community development. She has endowed three memorial scholarships in the C. T. Bauer College of Business at UH, the Lamar University College of Business in Beaumont, and the McCombs School of Business at the University of Texas, Austin, honoring her aunt, paternal grandparents, and parents.

She was a participant in the "Global Strategy Discussions" at the Naval War College, Newport, Rhode Island, and in 1976, she was invited to the White House to attend the International Women's Year report ceremony presentation to President Gerald R. Ford.

Dr. Stead developed a course called Marketing for Nonprofits; her students completed over 150 projects for Houston-area nonprofits. She chaired the $1.9 million renovation of Christ Church Cathedral (Episcopal, 1839) in Houston. For the Women's Home, she chaired task forces for the Adele and Ber Pieper Family Place (affordable housing) and Mabee WholeLife Service Center, $27 million; Jane Cizik Garden Place (affordable housing), $11 million; and Midtown Campus, treatment and transitional housing, capital expansion, $4.5 million.

She served as a docent at the Bayou Bend House Museum, Museum of Fine Arts, Houston (2003-2011) and board (2006-2007). She is married to C. Eugene Carlton, MD, distinguished professor emeritus, Scott Department of Urology, Baylor College of Medicine, Houston.